CANADA

by Susan Hoskins Miller

The Child's World

Published by The Child's World®
1980 Lookout Drive • Mankato, MN 56003-1705
800-599-READ • www.childsworld.com

Acknowledgments
The Child's World®: Mary Berendes, Publishing Director
Red Line Editorial: Editorial direction
The Design Lab: Design
Amnet: Production

Design elements: Shutterstock Images; iStockphoto
Photographs ©: iStock/Thinkstock, cover (right), 30;
iStockphoto, cover (left center), 1 (bottom left), 6–7, 10,
17 (left), 26; Shutterstock Images, cover (left bottom), cover
(left top), 1 (top), 1 (bottom right), 8, 17 (right), 19, 21,
22–23, 24, 28; Chris Hill/Shutterstock Images, 5; Al Parker
Photography/Shutterstock Images, 11; Benoit Daoust/
Shutterstock Images, 12, 25; Julien Hautcoeur/Shutterstock
Images, 13; Kiev Victor/Shutterstock Images, 16

ISBN 9781634070393
LCCN 2014959734

Printed in the United States of America
Mankato, MN
July, 2015
PA02268

ABOUT THE AUTHOR

Susan Hoskins Miller enjoys writing about places and people. She has written for numerous magazines, newspapers, and websites. She lives near Indianapolis, Indiana, where she works in a university library and can look up anything she wants to know about Canada.

ONE WORLD • MANY COUNTRIES •

TABLE OF CONTENTS

ARCTIC
OCEAN

CANADA

ATLANTIC
OCEAN

PACIFIC
OCEAN

PACIFIC
OCEAN

INDIAN
OCEAN

SCALE

0   1000 Miles

0   1000 KM

N
W   E
S

SOUTHERN
OCEAN

FUN FACT

The border between
Canada and the United
States is 5,525 miles
(8,892 km) long. It is
the world's longest
border between two
countries.

CANADA

ONE WORLD. ONE COUNTRIES

WELCOME TO CANADA!

In New Brunswick, Canada, people waited and watched on the shore of the Petitcodiac River on July 24, 2013. Two surfers were about to surf the river's waves. No one had ever tried it before. Most rivers do not have waves big enough to surf.

The surfers carried their surfboards into the water. They hopped on the huge wave coming at them. They stood up and surfed. Cheers came from the crowd. The surfers rode that wave for 10 miles (16 km). Then they caught another wave.

The Petitcodiac River is calm in many areas. When the river nears the Bay of Fundy, the large waves begin.

The men ended up surfing for 18 miles (29 km) that day. It took them two and a half hours. When they were done, they were shocked by how they looked. They were covered in mud.

The Petitcodiac River is very muddy. Its nickname is the Chocolate River. Word spread fast about the big waves on the Chocolate River. Now surfers come to surf the Chocolate River all the time.

The Petitcodiac River has waves big enough to surf on because it flows into the Bay of Fundy. The Bay of Fundy has the world's highest tides. They push into the river, creating large waves.

The Petitcodiac River flows through the large country of Canada. This country has huge mountains. It has acres of forests. Canada has the most lakes in the world. It has the largest French-speaking city outside of Paris, France.

In Canada people have French, English, and Scottish roots. Native people called Inuit live there, too. Together, all these people have created a nation unlike any other.

Many people enjoy surfing on Canada's rivers and oceans.

CHAPTER 2

THE LAND

Northern Lights glow brightly in Canada's night sky. Northern Lights are arcs of color that only occur near Earth's poles.

Canada is in North America. It is the second-largest country in the world. Only Russia is bigger. To its south, Canada borders the United States. The United States is Canada's only neighbor. Oceans form the rest of Canada's borders. On its eastern side is the Atlantic Ocean. The Pacific Ocean forms Canada's western border. The Arctic Ocean is to Canada's north.

The land in northern Canada stretches into the **Arctic Circle**. It is near the North Pole. This part of Canada is home to 36,000 islands. Canada has other islands, too. They are in the Atlantic and Pacific oceans. These islands give Canada more miles of coast than any country in the world.

Several mountain ranges tower across Canada. The Appalachian Mountains are in eastern Canada. The Rocky Mountains run along Canada's western side. The highest peak in the Canadian Rockies is Mount Robson. It is 2,972 feet (3,954 m) tall.

The mountains give way to prairies. They are in central Canada. Almost all of this land is used for farming. Farmers grow wheat, oats, and barley. Cattle are raised here, too.

Canada has more lakes than all the world's other countries put together. No one knows how many there are for sure. Officials have counted nearly 3 million lakes.

Canada shares four of the Great Lakes with the United States. The two countries also share Niagara Falls. These waterfalls form the border between Ontario, Canada, and the state of New York. Many people visit the falls each year.

The Niagara River has three major waterfalls. They are the Horseshoe Falls (above), American Falls, and Bridal Veil Falls.

The climate in Canada varies greatly between the north and south. In the north, winters are long and bitterly cold. Summers are cool and short. In the south, Canada has hot, humid summers. The winters are cold and snowy.

When the United States has an endangered species, it often calls Canada for help so the animal does not become extinct. Canada has sent grey wolves to Yellowstone National Park and wood bison to Alaska from their homes in Alberta.

FUN FACT

ONE WORLD · MANY COUNTRIES

5 CANADA

Fish are an important resource in Canada. Canadians sell their fish to other countries. Another important resource in Canada is **timber**. Almost half of Canada's land is covered with trees. Lumberjacks cut down the trees and send them to mills. Much of the wood is used to make lumber and paper.

A Canadian lumberjack cuts down a tree.

CHAPTER 3

GOVERNMENT AND CITIES

Canada's parliament building is on the banks of the Rideau Canal in Ottawa.

Ottawa, Ontario, is the capital of Canada. That is where the country's government meets. Canada is a democracy. That means its citizens can vote for their leaders and lawmakers.

A prime minister leads Canada and its government. The country's laws are made by members of **parliament**. Canada also has a governor general. The governor general's role is **ceremonial.**

These leaders govern Canada's ten **provinces**. Provinces are like states in the United States. Each province has a government, which makes local laws.

Canada also has three **territories**. They are in northern Canada. Unlike the provinces, the territories do not have local governments. Canada's national government makes all the laws for the territories.

Most Canadians live in southern Canada. Toronto is the largest city in Canada. Close to 5.6 million people live there. The city has many natural resources, such as minerals, timber, and water. Many businesses, banks, and factories are located there.

Toronto is often used by Hollywood producers as a place to make movies. Canada charges moviemakers lower taxes than U.S. cities charge. And, Toronto city streets and buildings can be changed a little to look like New York or Chicago streets.

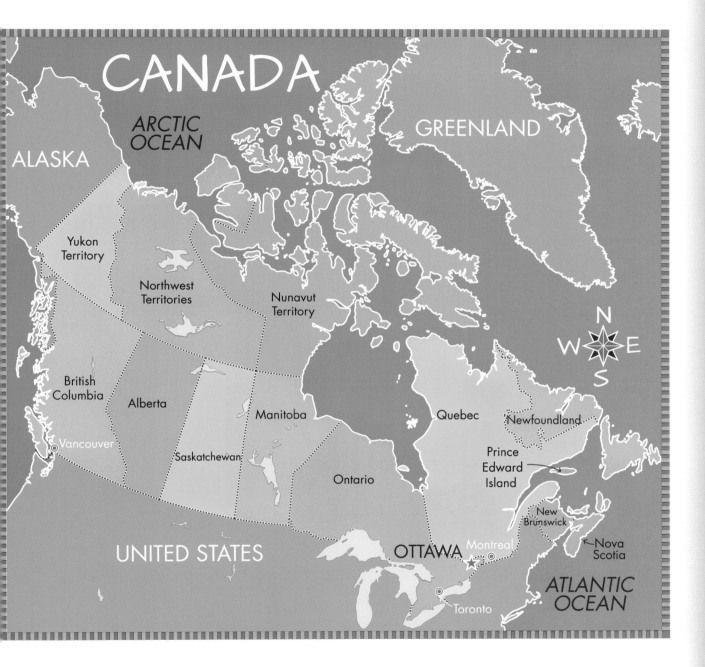

CANADA

ARCTIC OCEAN

GREENLAND

ALASKA

Yukon Territory

Northwest Territories

Nunavut Territory

N
W E
S

British Columbia

Alberta

Manitoba

Saskatchewan

Quebec

Newfoundland

Vancouver

Ontario

Prince Edward Island

New Brunswick

Nova Scotia

UNITED STATES

OTTAWA

Montreal

Toronto

ATLANTIC OCEAN

The Canadian National Tower rises above the Toronto skyline.

Many people who visit Toronto go to see the Canadian National Tower. This is the tallest building in Canada. It is 1,815 feet (553 m) tall. Inside is an elevator with a glass floor. People can look down and see how high off the ground they are.

Montreal is the second largest city in Canada. This city was built by French settlers. Today, most of the people who live in Montreal speak French. The buildings in the city look like they came from France.

Before the American colonies became the United States of America in 1776, Canada and the United States were both under British rule. So when Benjamin Franklin set up the postal system, he set it up for both the United States and Canada. Both countries still use the basic system Franklin designed.

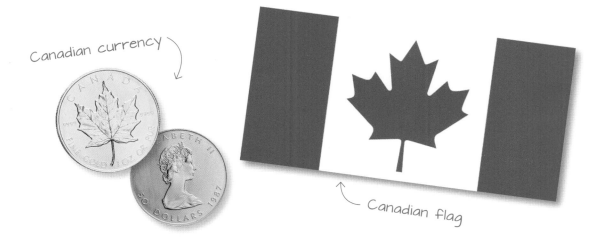

Canadian currency

Canadian flag

GLOBAL CONNECTIONS

Canada is known throughout the world for its maple trees and the syrup they produce. Almost 85 percent of the world's maple syrup comes from Canada. The country ships its syrup to the United States and many other countries.

Canada's shipping partners are the United States, China, and the United Kingdom. Besides maple syrup, Canada also ships wood from its forests to other countries.

Canada buys goods from the United States, China, and Mexico. It is joining the Pacific Alliance to grow its shipping trade. The Pacific Alliance is a group of countries that have joined together to make it easier to ship products to each other. The countries all border the Pacific Ocean.

Canada lets some people from other countries come to live there. About 600,000 people from other countries come to Canada to live every year. Some are students and workers. They may only stay for a few years. Then many go back to their home countries to live. But many other people stay in Canada.

CHAPTER 4

PEOPLE AND CULTURES

A girl performs a dance at a Native American festival in Ontario.

Many people of different cultures have settled in Canada over time. Native Americans were some of the first people who lived there. The Inuit people settled in Canada many years ago. They live in the cold areas of the north.

European settlers came next. They arrived from Scotland, England, and France. They started businesses that used Canada's minerals, timber, and furs. Today, many Canadians can trace their roots back to these European settlers.

Canada has two official languages. They are English and French. Most French speakers live in the province of Quebec. English is the main language in the other provinces and territories. Many Inuit people also continue to speak their native language.

Canadians like to celebrate holidays. Canada Day is on July 1. It is the day the Constitution Act of 1867 was signed. This act made Canada a country. Before that, Canada had been a territory belonging to England. People go to parades, picnics, and fireworks.

Canada's Thanksgiving is the second Monday of October. The Thanksgiving feast is like the one in the United States. People eat roast turkey, stuffing, and pumpkin pie. They give thanks for the good things in their lives.

Victoria Day honors the birthday of England's late Queen Victoria. It is usually a three-day weekend toward the end of May.

This Canadian soldier is wearing a traditional Scottish kilt and playing the bagpipes, a Scottish instrument.

For Canadians, it is the official start of summer. People celebrate with barbecues, fireworks, picnics, and outdoor activities. Many Canadians celebrate religious holidays, too, such as Christmas and Easter.

Different festivals are held in Canada. Toronto has a film festival in September. Quebec holds a yearly Winter Carnival. The Inuit have a festival that celebrates their **ancestors**. Quebec has French holidays, such as Saint-Jean-Baptiste Day. Other nationalities in Canada host festivals and holidays that honor their different cultures.

A canoe race takes place in the icy waters of the St. Lawrence River during Quebec's Winter Carnival.

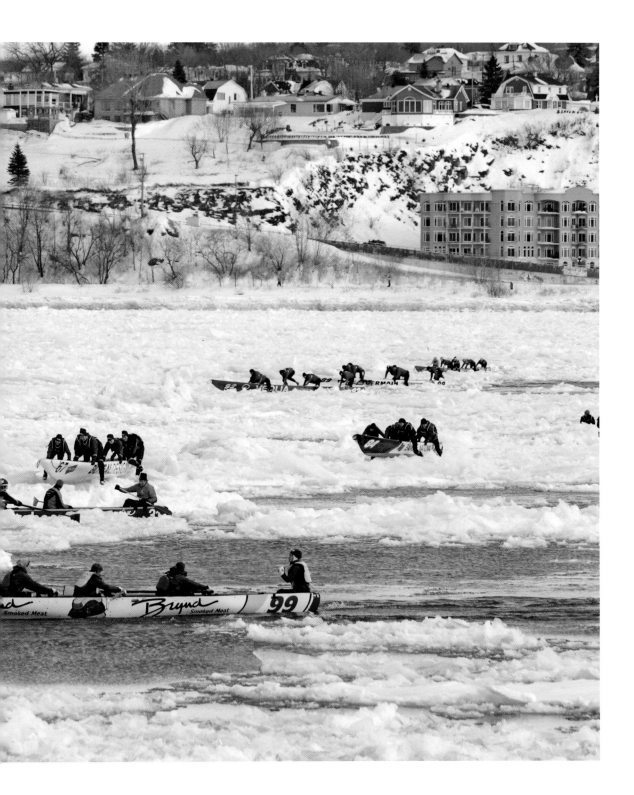

Quebec's Winter Carnival is held in February. The carnival includes ice sculptures, sleigh races, snow baths, and parades. A giant snowman is a mascot for the carnival. His name is Bonhomme Carnaval.

FUN FACT

ONE WORLD · MANY COUNTRIES

CANADA

CHAPTER 5

DAILY LIFE

A team of three snowplows works to clear a highway in Montreal. Driving during Canada's icy, snowy winters is difficult.

Winter is cold and snowy in Canada. Toronto and Montreal have long tunnels underground. This allows people to walk places without having to go out in bad weather. Many Canadians use buses and trains. It is easier than driving their own cars on snowy city streets.

Many places in Canada are similar to those in the United States. The cities look alike. Small towns and farm life is so much like the northern United States that one can hardly tell the difference.

Sports are an important part of Canadian culture. Many Canadians love hockey more than any other sport. Canadian kids play hockey on frozen ponds during the winters. Hockey games are on television every Saturday night during the hockey season.

FUN FACT

ONE WORLD · MANY COUNTRIES

About 75 percent of Canadians live within 150 miles (241 km) of the U.S. border. That's because the weather along the border is much milder than that in the far north. Many cities near the border have also grown due to trade with the United States.

Many children in Canada play pond hockey in the winter.

A dog sled race during Quebec's Winter Carnival.

Because of cold temperatures, people must dress warmly when going outdoors in winter. Skin must be covered completely to avoid **frostbite**. Canadians dress in layers of clothing and wear warm boots.

Even in the cold, Canadians know how to enjoy the outdoors. They go sledding and snowmobiling. Some even go dog sledding. This is when a team of dogs works together to pull a sled across the ice and snow.

Canada is a country that is big and vast. It stretches from the United States all the way to the Arctic Circle. Canada is home to many kinds of people. Its wild areas have thick forests and frozen land. Yet this country also has cities full of art and culture. It is this wide variety that makes Canada a truly unique place.

DAILY LIFE FOR CHILDREN

In Canada, children begin school at age five. Parents can choose what type of school their children attend. They have the options of schools that teach lessons in English or French.

Sometimes in the winter, school is canceled. The days off are called snow days. Snow days happen when there has been a snowstorm, and the roads are too dangerous for driving. Children get to stay home and play.

The winter also means fun outside. Canadian children like to plays outdoor sports such as hockey and ringette. Like hockey, ringette players skate on ice. Instead of a hockey puck and stick, players use straight sticks and a blue rubber ring.

FAST FACTS

Population: 34 million

Area: 3,855,100 square miles (9,984,670 sq km)

Capital: Ottawa

Largest Cities: Toronto, Montreal, Quebec, and Vancouver

Form of Government: Parliamentary Democracy

Languages: English and French

Trading Partners: United States, United Kingdom, and China

Major Holidays: Canada Day, Victoria Day, Thanksgiving, Christmas, and Easter

National Dish: Poutine (French fries mixed with cheese curds and covered in a brown beef gravy)

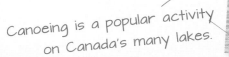

Canoeing is a popular activity on Canada's many lakes.

GLOSSARY

ancestors (AN-sess-turz) Ancestors are people who were part of a family many years ago. In Quebec, many people have French ancestors.

Arctic Circle (ARK-tic CIR-kul) The Arctic Circle is a frozen area near the North Pole. Northern Canada is in the Arctic Circle.

ceremonial (ser-uh-MO-ne-uhl) Ceremonial means having no real power. In Canada, the governor general's role is ceremonial.

frostbite (FRAWST-bite) Frostbite is a condition that happens when skin freezes after being exposed to cold temperatures. People in Canada wear warm clothes to prevent frostbite.

parliament (PAR-luh-ment) Parliament is a group that makes laws. The parliament in Canada makes the country's laws.

provinces (PRAH-vens-ez) Provinces are large areas that some countries are divided into. Canada has ten provinces.

territories (TEHR-uh-tor-ez) Territories are areas of land that are controlled by a government. Canada has three territories.

timber (TIM-bur) Timber describes trees that are grown to produce wood. Timber is an important part of Canada's economy.

TO LEARN MORE

BOOKS

Barlas, Robert. *Festivals of the World: Canada.* New York: Marshall Cavendish Benchmark, 2011.

McDonnell, Ginger. *Next Stop: Canada.* Huntington Beach, CA: Teacher Created Materials, 2011.

National Geographic Guide to the National Parks of Canada. Washington, DC: National Geographic, 2011.

WEB SITES

Visit our Web site for links about Canada: **childsworld.com/links**

Note to Parents, Teachers, and Librarians: We routinely verify our Web links to make sure they are safe and active sites. So encourage your readers to check them out!

INDEX